Dr. Marianne Stradal

NEEDLECRAFT

with beads
and crystals

Translated by H. Hertz
Dora Wirth (Languages) Ltd
London

MILLS & BOON LONDON

First published in English by
Mills & Boon Limited, 17-19 Foley Street,
London   W 1 A   1 D R

© this edition Mills & Boon Limited 1971

ISBN 0-263-05005-X

Printed in West Germany

CONTENTS

INTRODUCTION

Pearls and gemstones were prized from very early civilisations and we ourselves, for all our sophistication, are far from impervious to the charm of coloured beads and glistening crystals piled up in front of us. Anyone who has tried her hand at ornamenting fabric or at knitting with beads and stones, will quickly fall under their spell. As with most other hobbies, the desire to own the finished article is only part of the incentive. Most people enjoy using their hands, the more so when the work requires imagination and skill. Many people find an unexpected thrill in doing something creative.

Before we come to the scope and the techniques of work with beads and crystals, it may be of interest to take a quick look at the long history of our attractive material.

A SHORT HISTORY OF GEMS AND BEADS

The art of glassmaking was known to the ancients. Who made the first glass, and where, is a matter of some controversy. A charming story by Pliny, claiming that the Phoenicians stumbled across the process by accident, is now, alas, discounted. We know that the ancient Egyptians knew how to make glass, but glass ornaments have also been found on prehistoric sites in Europe. Graves of the La Tène and Later Hallstatt periods have yielded glass bracelets and ring beads, very small, thick rings, which were probably used for adornment but also valued as amulets. In describing them, a contemporary scientist developed a theory of Celtic glass.

Modern glass, including of course Bohemian glass, probably had its beginnings in Venice. We know quite a lot about its early days. We find, for instance, that as early as 1291, the glassmakers of Venice, because their work represented a fire hazard, were banished to the island of Murano, which has ever since been the home of the renowned Venetian glass, and of glass beads. Marco Polo, the famous traveller, was the son of a Venetian glassmaker. He used glass beads for barter in the exotic lands that he visited between 1300 and 1332.

The Venetians are credited with having introduced glass into England and many other countries of Europe, including Bohemia. Two glassmakers are said to have been murdered for betraying the secrets of their craft. The secrets for glassmaking have been jealously guarded for centuries. Some of the old reticence is still with us today, and we encounter it in a modern bead factory in Neugablonz no less than in Wattens, in the Tyrol, where world-famous synthetic gems are turned out. The founder of this company, the skyscrapers of which vie with the mountains surrounding them, emigrated four generations ago from Gablonz in Bohemia. He carried with him the secret processes involved in staining and polishing glass stones which were perfected away from the prying eyes of competitors, in the isolation of the Tyrolean mountains not yet discovered by tourists. The iridescent beads and stones, which catch and reflect every hue, have since conquered the world.

However, to return to the history of glass beads, — the dense forests of the Iser mountains, the most northerly part of the Sudetenland, favoured the establishment of glassworks. According to an old parish record from Schumburg, near Gablonz, the first glassworks were built there in 1414. Incidentally, one of the founder's descendants, one John Kittel, achieved a different sort of fame, as a quack. — Razed to the ground in the Hussite wars, Gablonz remained a backwoods village until 1539, but, together with the entire neighbourhood, it began to develop rapidly when the glassblowers attracted more skilled labour to the lonely virgin forests of the Iser mountains. The glass-cutting works were moved close to mountain streams. The history of what is now the city of Gablonz — a name synonymous with its industry — is in effect the history of the individual families that have advanced and developed their ancient craft from generation to generation. The making of beads, and later of jewellery, has always depended on the craftsman rather than the conveyor belt.

No less essential than the craftsmen were the busy glass merchants. These Bohemian successors to Marco Polo carried glass beads all over the world, as objects of barter and trade. The trade reached its supreme importance in the 18th and 19th century. Travellers who made contact with primitive societies soon discovered that the human desire for adornment is as old as the development of clothes as protection against the weather, or as a body covering. Bead necklaces took the place of necklaces made from nuts or animal teeth, and in some African tribes, represented the sole attire of the local belles. American Indians abandoned their intricate embroidery with stained wild pig bristles and took to decorating their moccasins with Bohemian glass beads. Examples of this work are still found in museums.

The merchants returned home with new impressions and conveyed the wishes of their customers from the whole wide world. Towards the end of the 18th century, the demand was not only for loose beads but also for beads set in metal. This was the beginning of the Gablonz jewellery industry. The beadmakers joined forces with the makers of belts and buckles, whose ancient craft was no less steeped in symbolism than its products. The coloured stones ornamenting the belts were often regarded as sources of life and vigour.

Costume jewellery is short-lived. Bought in the autumn, it is forgotten by summer. The trade must think up novelties for every new season. Creating new fashions is not the prerogative of great designers. Actresses do their share. Sarah Bernhardt had the bodices of her dresses embroidered with gems and pearls, and transplanted the fashion to the other side of the footlights. Gaby Deslys, the toast of Paris about the turn of the century, used to make her entrance in a huge hat, plastered with beads and crystals, which she

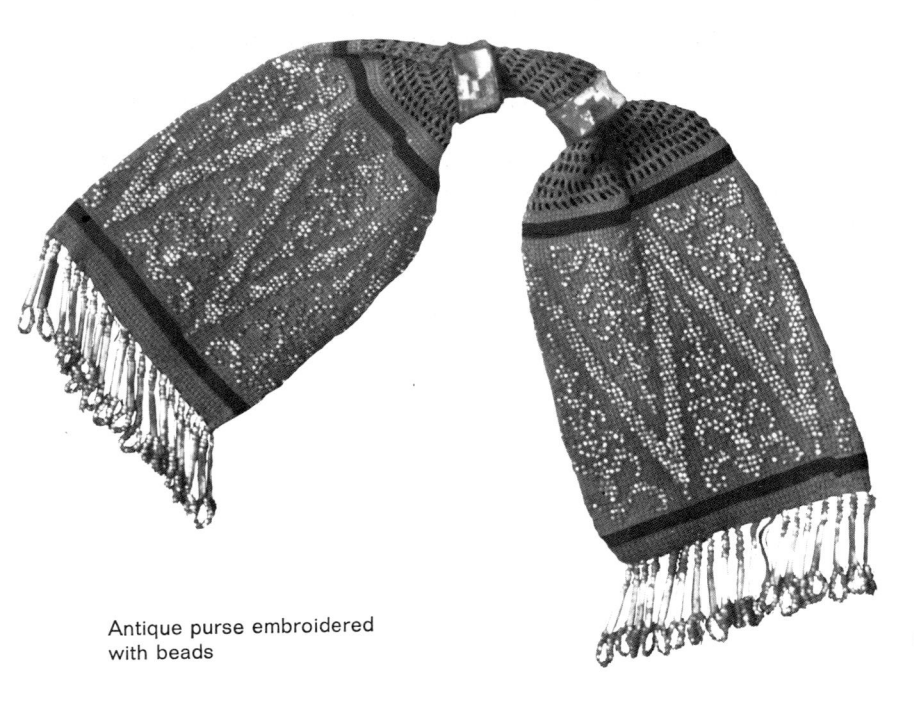

Antique purse embroidered
with beads

then flung on to an ever-present chaise longue. That too caught on, and every fine lady's hat was weighted down with beads and brooches. Not that Gaby was the first woman to launch a fashion in hats. In 1371, the Duke of Burgundy presented his beautiful duchess with a hat decorated with 600 large pearls and 50 ounces of small pearls. As Burgundy was then the Mecca of the fashionable world, the hat was not long unique.

The beadmakers of the Fichtel mountains in Germany specialised in rosary beads. Theirs were glass beads, but the rosaries of earlier days were often made of amber, or precious stones or real pearls. A rosary given by the Emperor Ferdinand to his daughter consisted of 90 gold beads.

The Emperor Francis, consort of Austria's Maria Theresa, was a quiet, simple man but he loved to wear pearls and gems, especially on his shoes. — The ceremonial gowns of royalty used to be embroidered with pearls and precious stones. To mention two famous examples: the Hungarian coronation robe embroidered in a 9th century convent in Stuhlweissenburg, and a gown ordered, several centuries later, by a Medici princess for the christening of her son. It was ornamented with 3200 pearls and 3000 diamonds and it is sad to relate that when the magnificent garment was finished, it proved much too heavy to wear.

As the taste for fashion and finery became more popular, costume jewellery came into its own. The Emperor Francis might wear real pearls on his shoes but his subjects were getting busy with beads and imitation stones. As time went on, real pearls were joined by cultured pearls and finally by imitation pearls. made by dipping glass beads into a solution of fish scales. Up to the end of World War I, imitation diamonds or other artificial gemstones were contemptuously dismissed as „paste", and no aspiring lady would be seen wearing them. But the same ladies' daughters, dancing the Charleston in the 1920s, would have felt naked without a hip-length string of glass beads over their short chemisetype dresses, which in turn were encrusted with round beads and tube-shaped beads like an 1870ish lampshade.

In ornamental needlework, beads had long been respectable. The value of glass beads in embroidery is said to have been discovered, early in the 19th century, by some Viennese ladies who decided that they could no longer afford the high price of silks. They bought cheap Bohemian beads and used them to embroider their rosebuds and daisies.

Bead knitted
christening bonnet

The idea caught on and spread quickly across Europe. Within a few years, bead embroidery had reached a standard that has never since been equalled. And an enterprising knitter had the idea of stringing beads on her thread and knitting them into a pattern. This beadknitting technique produced some very fine purses, christening bonnets and bags, examples of endless patience and high degree of skill. Bead needle-weaving and bead weaving on small looms also belong to this period.

Some fashion designers of the 20th century, such as Coco Chanel and Elsa Schiaparelli, created the concept of clothes and jewellery as a single unit. In a way, they form a link with the Renaissance, where painters learned from fashion designers and vice versa. For instance, a pearl tiara would match the entire style of a gown decorated all over with pearls and smocking. The gowns of the Renaissance lead us to the Haute Couture of today which freely uses beads and coloured glass. This has led to a revival of interest in embroidery with beads and crystals. Thousands of colourful beads and shimmering crystals are being used with great skill in modern needlework. This booklet is intended to help others to take up this enjoyable and creative hobby and, who knows, it may even suggest a new idea or two to those who have already fallen victim to the spell of beadcraft.

Bead purse
early 19th century

NEEDLECRAFT WITH BEADS

Bead Embroidery

The most important tool for bead embroidery is a sewing needle which must be fine enough to pass through the often tiny hole in the beads. As the eyes of such needles are inevitably small, a threader is essential. The third important item is a thimble.

The thread for bead embroidery should be very strong and long-lasting; at the same time, it has to be fine enough. This makes one of the man-made fibres an obvious choice.

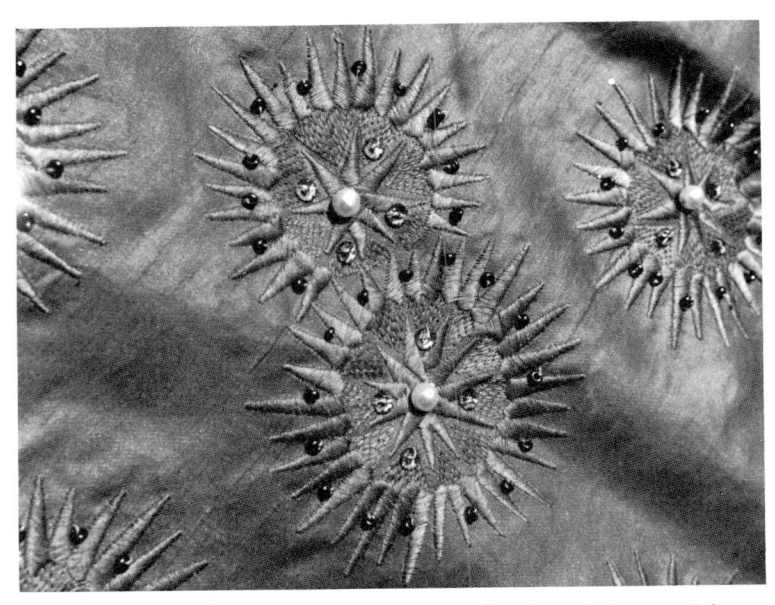

Machine embroidered silk fabric decorated with beads and glass crystals

13

Patterned or embroidered fabrics can be greatly enriched by the addition of beads. Beads placed on the petals or sepals of flowers, for instance, can look like dewdrops. Special effects may be obtained by combining beads with coloured crystals. More of this later (illustration on p. 13).

The basic fabric for bead embroidery may be plain or patterned. A patterned background does not call for quite so much imagination or draughtsmanship, as this part of the work will have largely been done by the designer of the fabric. Additional aids may be provided by speciality weaving, or machine embroidery.

Plain fabrics call for a design, and this represents a much greater challenge. It is a good idea to take a cutting of material and experiment with a few beads, to see what they will look like arranged in a particular design. This is particularly helpful if it is proposed to use beads of different sizes and colours. The design should then be transferred to paper. It is sufficient to indicate the various kinds of beads by different types of dots.

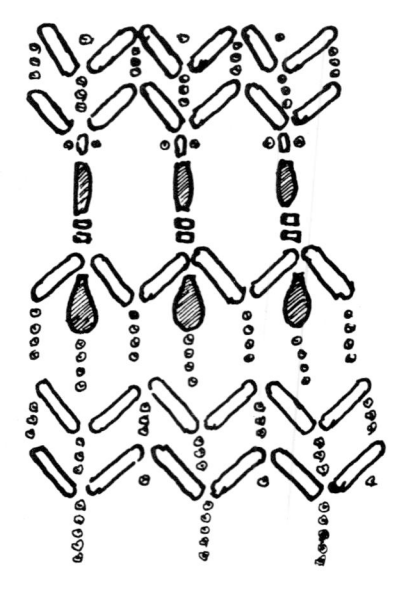

clear glass

light purple

dark purple

white

The design may then be transferred to the fabric by pouncing or by special transfer paper, and the actual embroidery can then begin. The photograph above shows the effect that can be obtained by using light purple and dark purple beads on a purple ground, and by varying small beads with larger, oblong ones. When using the longer beads, it is particularly important to get the tension of the thread exactly right, neither too loose nor too taut, and to have the bead in the required position before the stitch is completed. On the wrong side, the length of stitches between beads must not be too long as the thread might break, or pull the fabric out of shape. It is usually advisable to line an embroidered fabric, say an evening dress or a belt, after the work is completed. The wrong side will then look tidy and the stitches will be protected.

In the 19th century, bead embroidery was not confined to clothes but was used to decorate all sorts of small articles. Purses, bags and other containers were particularly favoured. An attractive example is shown below. It is an embroidered tatting bag from the 1880s — tatting was the fashionable craze of the period. The

Embroidered
tatting bag

dainty bag contained the unfinished work together with the shuttle — which might be of ivory or even gold — and accompanied its owner everywhere, even when she went visiting.

In a very special type of bead embroidery, beads cover the entire surface. Here the beads are not spaced out to decorate an existing fabric; instead, each bead forms a dot in a stippled picture. As in the case of canvas work or needle tapestry, the design is first marked out on canvas and then worked in much the same way, except that each stitch applies one bead. The designs too are those of traditional canvas work. First petals and leaves are embroidered with beads of different shades, and then the background is filled in with black beads. The material, that is, beads, marked canvas, prepared lining and so on may be obtained in complete kits. This form of bead embroidery calls for patience and skilled workmanship but it is also rewarding (illustrations opposite).

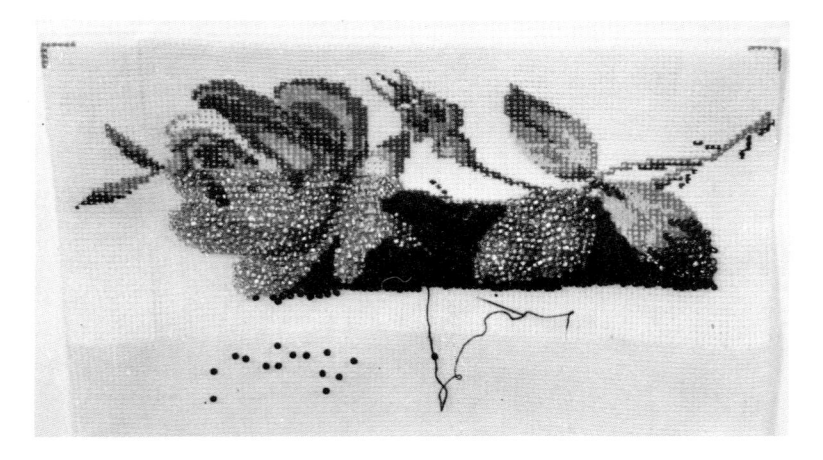

Bead embroidery of rose design
marked out on canvas

Handbag, entire surface
embroidered with beads

17

Bead knitting

Bead knitting is another revival of an early 19th century craft. Now as then, handbags are the articles most favoured.

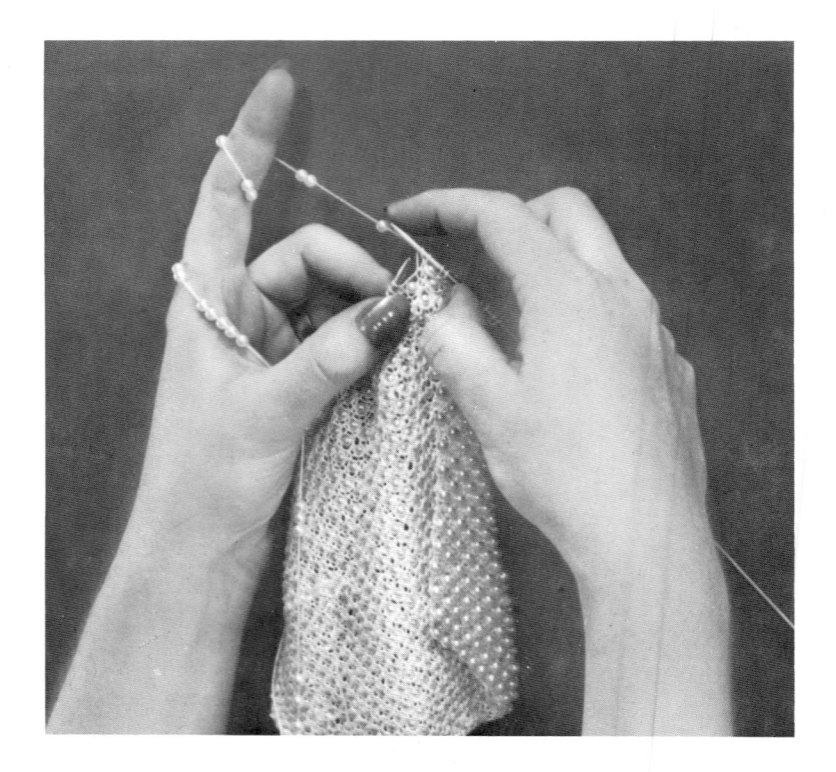

The first step is to thread the beads on the knitting yarn. Knitting can then begin. For greater control of the beads it is recommended to knit in the Continental style with the wool to the left (see illustration). Use the index finger of the right hand to guide the bead between the stitch just completed and the one about to be knitted. The bead is then fixed on what for this row is the wrong side, in other words, away from you. The next row is generally knitted without beads. The row after that is again knitted with beads, with the beads moved along one stitch so as to produce a diagonal line. Where beads of only one colour are used, as shown here, the design, that is the number of rows and stitches between beads, may of course be varied to suit individual tastes.

The evening handbag illustrated has a matching purse and spectacle case. This too is supplied in complete kits consisting of beads, knitting yarn, pre-sewn lining and frame together with detailed instructions. For those who prefer to work more independently, a wide choice of beads, frames etc can be obtained as separate items.

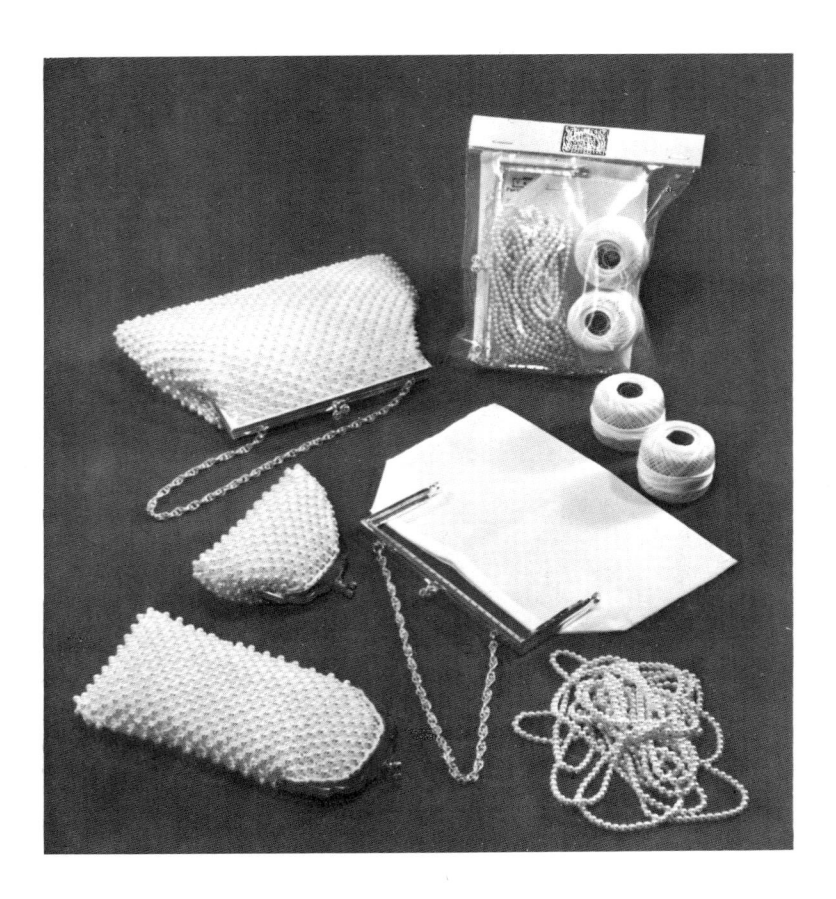

White beads are used for the evening bag on p. 19 which is worked as follows:

Size 12 or 14 needles are recommended (USA 1 or 00).
Thread half the beads, about 300, on one ball of yarn, and the remainder on the other ball. The entire bag is knitted plain.
Cast on 28 stitches.
Row 1: Knit (plain).
Rows 2, 4 and 6 (bead rows): Knit 2, guide 1 bead to face away from you. Repeat to end of row.
Rows 3, 5 and 7: Knit (plain) and increase by 1 stitch at each end.
Row 8: As Row 6.
Row 9: Knit plain.
Row 10: Knit 1, insert 1 bead (so that beads move up one) then as Row 8. Continue in this way (bead rows 6 and 10 alternately) up to and including Row 54.
Row 55: Knit plain. Decrease by 1 stitch at both ends.
Rows 56, 58 and 60: as Row 8.
Rows 57, 59 and 61: As Row 55.
Row 62: Cast off loosely.
Finishing: Fold and stitch edges together alongside beads, up to the point of decrease. Stitch to frame from the right side. Sew in lining.

Purse and spectacle case may be knitted in the same way, apart from the obvious differences in size and number of rows. Full instructions are supplied with each kit.

Similar kits are available for a wide variety of bags, and with black, gold, iridescent beads etc. Small purses to contain change for parking meters can be knitted with green, red or blue beads.

Evening bags may also be knitted with sequins in place of beads. These sequins are much larger than those of an earlier fashion. With their iridescent gold colour, they make elegant evening bags.

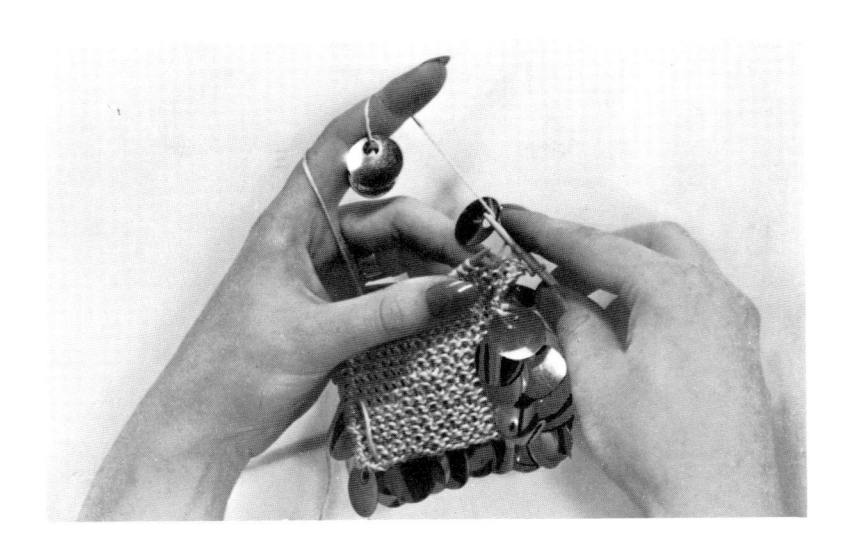

Evening bag with
knitted-in sequins

Enterprising knitters are even using beads for pullovers and tops. Such garments have a timeless beauty not easily affected by day-to-day changes in fashion.

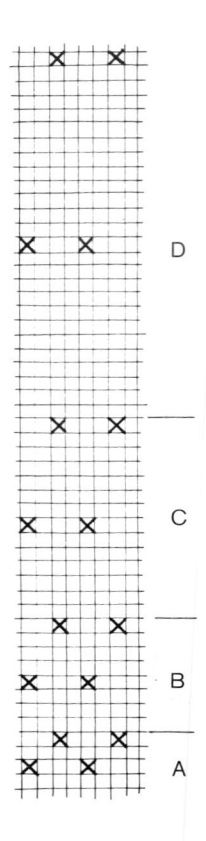

The jumper illustrated shows varied spacings of beads on a stocking stitch ground (knit 1 row, purl 1 row). For this pattern, work A 5 times (each x represents a bead) B 5 times, C 5 times and D 3 times. The neckband is also knitted in stocking stitch, and beginning with Row 18, pattern A is incorporated 3 times. Fine, single-shade wool should be used, for instance navy or black, with small, silver grey or white beads. 130 grammes (about 4½ ounces) of small beads are required for this design.

Another design that will weather many a fashion change — stylised vine leaves of white beads against a red background.

This jumper too is knitted in stocking stitch. The motifs appear at regular intervals but transposed. Each leaf motif is 19 stitches wide and 16 stitches high; the distances between motifs are 21 stitches. The beads are threaded on the wool in the usual way. Each motif incorporates 129 beads.

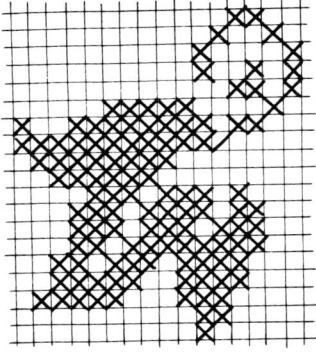

23

Cardigans too may be decorated with beads, for instance, on the front edges. Orange beads against a charcoal grey background form an effective contrast.

Knitted bead border

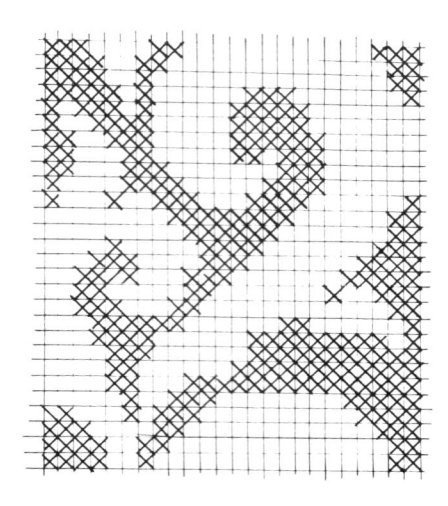

The two bead borders are knitted separately and joined to the cardigan later. Here again, needless to say, the beads have first to be threaded. Knit 1 row, purl 1 row, as shown in the pattern.

Multi-coloured rose motifs are among the most versatile ornaments but they require the same standards of workmanship displayed by the more leisured ladies of the 1820s.

First the beads have to be threaded in exactly the right sequence of the colours shown in the pattern. This requires careful counting and stringing before knitting can even begin.

For the small rose motive, follow the direction of arrow B.

> 1st row: (wrong side) purl 13, then purl 4 with 1 dark green bead behind each stitch. Purl 9.
>
> 2nd row: Knit plain.
>
> 3rd row: Purl 15. The next two purled stitches are each follow-ed by 1 dark green bead. Purl 2, purl the next 4 with 1 light green bead after each stitch. Purl 1, 1 red bead, purl 2.
>
> 4th row: Knit plain.

Continue through pattern.

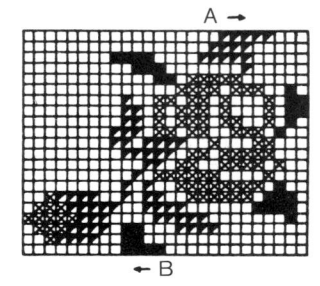

■· light green

■· dark green

▨· red

As it would be too difficult to thread all the beads for the entire motif at once, it is recommended to string the beads for 4 rows, then to break the thread and to begin again. This method has the additional advantage of allowing the correction of possible errors in the colour sequence.

Bead crocheting

Summer handbag in
beaded crochetwork

Crocheting with beads follows the same principle as knitting with beads. Here too, the beads have first to be threaded and each bead is then pulled into place between two stitches with the crochet hook. In this pretty summer handbag, the beads are fitted between simple shell patterns over the entire surface of the bag.

Use a size 7 (4.5 International) crochet hook. About half the total number of beads should be threaded on to mercerised cotton for the first part of the work. The thread bearing the other half can be joined later.

The work is begun in the centre of the base. Crochet three rows of the chain, then continue the next rows in the round up to the opening.

Begin with a chain of 43 stitches.

1st row: Work 5 trebles into the 4th chain, (+) miss 2 chains, work 2 double crochet through the next chain with the bead between. Miss 2 chains, 5 trebles into the next chain. Repeat from (+) to the end of the row. The row, which will consist of 7 shells, should end in 1 double crochet without a bead.

2nd row: 3 chains to turn, 2 Tr into DC of last row (+), 1 DC, bead, 1 DC into 3rd Tr of last row, 5 trebles between the 2 DC of last row. Continue from (+) to end of row, ending with 3 Tr.

3rd row: I ch for turning (+), 5 Tr between 2 DC of last row, 1 DC, 1 bead, 1 DC into 3 rd Tr. Continue from (+) to end of row, ending with 1 DC without bead.

Repeat the first row on the other side of the chain, working trebles and double crochets through the same chains as before but leave out the beads. Work the next two rows exactly as above.

The base of the bag is now finished and we continue in the round, beginning in the centre of one of the narrow sides: —

1st row: 1 DC, 1 bead, 1 DC into the first ch, 5 Tr into DC of previous row to form corner. (+) 1 DC, 1 bead, 1 DC into 3rd Tr, 5 Tr between 2 DC of last row, continue from (+) to next corner, 5 Tr into the last DC. 1 DC into last stitch of chain on the other narrow side, 1 bead, 1 DC. Continue second half of round exactly as the first half. End round, which should contain 16 shells, with a chain stitch.

2nd and 3rd rounds are worked exactly as the 2nd and 3rd round of the base, only in the round. End with chain stitches.

4th to 18th row: Continue the interchange as with 2nd and 3rd row.

To finish: Complete kits are again available, containing cotton, beads, made-up lining and frame. The lining is affixed to the penultimate row. The staves of the frame at both sides are passed through the middle 6 shells of the penultimate row. This leaves 3 shells to make the sides so that the bag may be opened.

(Chain-stitch = ch; Treble = Tr, Double crochet = DC)

The same technique could be applied to the neck of a jumper. Jumper and handbag may be worked in matching colour schemes. Bead crochetwork is also suitable for the hem, say 6 inches, of a summer skirt. A skirt may also be crocheted in raffia. It should be borne in mind, though, that the threading of beads on raffia presents considerable difficulty and the work should only be attempted with wooden beads, with large holes.

A beaded edge can make all the difference to a small crochet collar.

A useful colour scheme would be turquoise wool or manmade fibre with a silver Lurex thread and 36 medium sized imitation pearls. 1 ball of silver crochet yarn is also required. Use a No. 11 crochet hook.

Begin with a chain of 52 stitches.

1st row: 2 ch for turning, (+) 1 DC into the 3rd ch, loop thread round hook as if for treble crochet, draw through 2 loops only, leaving 2 on the hook. Loop again, hook into the same stitch and draw thread through all the loops on the hook. Miss 1 ch, repeat from (+).

2nd to 6th rows: As 1st row, but work DC into the stitch that pulls together the group from the last row.

After these 6 rows, thread the 36 beads on the silver yarn and work the edging as follows: —

1 DC, 1 ch, 1 bead between this and next ch, 2 DC, 1 ch, 1 bead, 1 ch, 2 DC etc.

Continue along outer edge of collar. Always pull the second chain-stitch so tight that the bead faces upwards.

If a wider border, or a collar and cuffs, are to be worked with small glistening beads, the holes of which are too small to allow threading on the man-made fibre used here, the beads may be strung on to silver crochet yarn. The silver yarn and the ordinary working thread are then crocheted together, and the beads are inserted where required. We suggest the following pattern: —

Work a chain.
1st row: 1 Tr into 3rd ch, (+), miss 2 ch, 1 DC into next ch, 3 ch, 1 Tr into the first of these 3 ch, repeat from (+);
1 Tr into chain-stitches, repeat from (+)
2nd row: 2 ch for turning, 1 DC into 2nd ch of arc underneath 1 bead, (+) 3 ch, 1 Tr into first of these 3 ch, 1 DC into the middle ch of next arc, insert bead, repeat from (+);
3rd row: as 2nd row, but without beads;
4th row: as 2nd row (with beads);
5th row: as 3rd row;
6th row: as 2nd row but insert 1 bead after the 2 ch, so that this final row is decorated with double the number of beads.

A very decorative narrow border can be worked with silver thread and glistening beads only. Begin as usual by threading the beads and then work a chain of the length required.

> 1st row: 1 ch for turning, (+) 1 DC into next ch, 1 ch, insert bead, miss 1 ch, 1 DC into next ch, 1 ch, miss 1 ch, repeat from (+).
> 2nd row: 2 ch for turning, (+) 1 DC into DC immediately below, 1 ch, repeat from (+);
> 3rd row: as 1st row but beads are moved up one.
> 4th row: as 2nd row;
> 5th row: as 1st row;
> 6th row: as 2nd row.

These three examples form only a fraction of the methods by which traditional crochetwork can be enriched by the addition of beads.

NEEDLE WEAVING WITH BEADS

This work requires no fabric base. The beads are fastened together with a stout thread, in carefully worked out sequences and techniques. Some schools are again teaching this old craft which is gaining in popularity.

Necklaces, belts and bracelets can be made from beads in a kind of weaving technique, though the only tools required are a bead needle (a long, thin needle) and very strong, fine thread of top quality pure silk or nylon. The number of beads will obviously depend on the nature of the article.

Swiss embroidery enriched with crystals.
Each crystal is stitched into the ▶
centre of a lace flower.

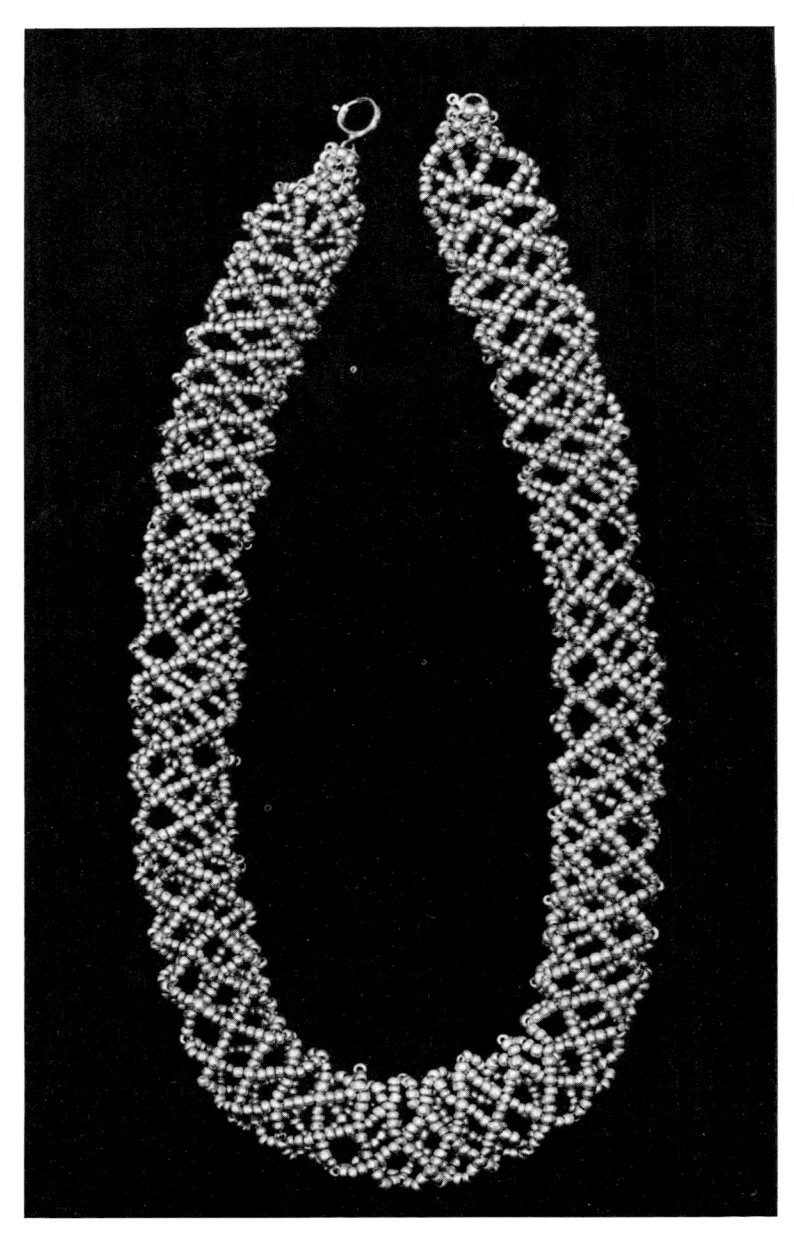

Necklace of intricate beadwork   33

A cardigan of shimmering Bri-Nylon.
Knitted in rose pattern, embroidered with sequin rosettes.
Large paillette buttons.

Needle weaving may be carried out with beads of one colour or of many colours. It is advisable for a beginner to work in one colour only until she masters the technique. Needle weaving can best be picked up by following step-by-step instructions. The directions given below are for a flat band of beads, and a round rope.

Instructions for the band

Bands require an even number of beads, in this case, 12. The thread should be roughly 40" long.

Thread 12 beads, plus 1. The first bead should be secured to the end of the thread (a). The last, that is, the 13th bead really belongs to the next row. — Draw the needle through the third bead from the end (b). Now take up every bead shown black on the diagram. Take up a new bead, draw the needle through the next bead but one, and continue in the same way to the end of the row. Pull the thread taut (c).

There will now be 6 beads on a higher and 6 on a lower level. Turn the work. The first bead of each row will be on the lower, and the last bead of each row on the higher level. Take up new bead, draw needle through the next upper level bead. Repeat 5 times to the end of the row. Pull thread tight (d). Turn work.

At the beginning of each row, it helps to hold work and thread firmly between index finger and thumb so that the first bead — the last of the previous row — is not pulled up. Any looseness or unevenness spoils the effect.

Begin next row and continue as before.

If a multi-coloured design has been selected, this should start after about an inch or just under. When you get to the end of your thread, join it to a fresh one by knotting. The two ends should be left not less than 3" long. Always join threads in the middle of a row (e). Use a slip knot and, with the aid of a pin, ease it close to the nearest bead (f). Leave the ends until you join the next thread, then use the needle to draw the ends through the adjacent beads to hide them. The ends must never be cut off or the knot will come undone.

The band can be finished either with a bead fringe, or a diagonal border, or the ends can be joined (p. 32).

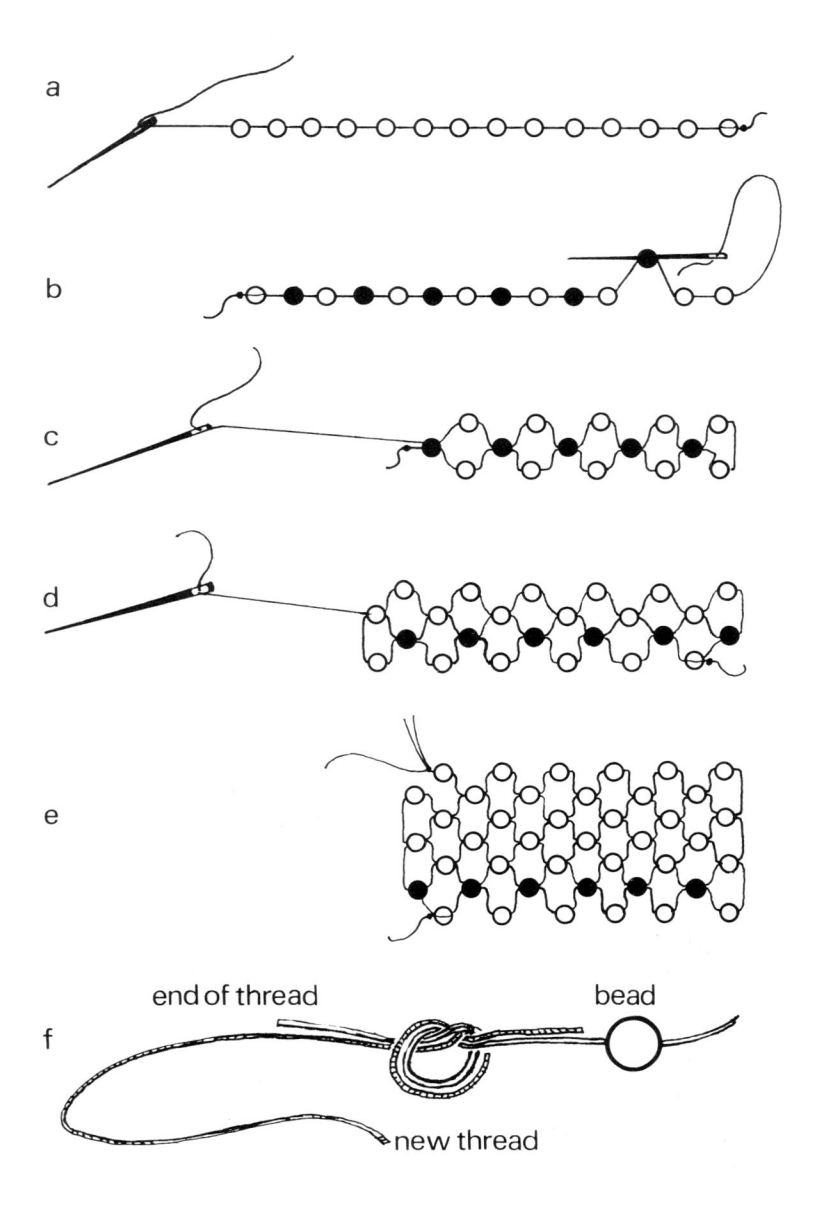

a

b

c

d

e

f

end of thread   bead

new thread

Instructions for a rope of beads

Take an uneven number of beads. The thread should be about 40" long.

Thread 13 beads. Secure the first one to the end of the thread. Draw the needle once more through the first bead. This will make a circle. Take up a new bead, draw needle through the next bead but one and repeat. Continue in the same way and draw thread tight after each round. Designs can obviously be made up by the use of different coloured beads.

Finish off with a necklace clasp or, if the rope is long enough to slip over the head, the ends may be joined. Alternatively, bead fringes may be used at both ends.

Design and Colour

It is useful to have some graph paper and coloured pencils to match the beads.

For a beadwork band, one takes an even number of beads, say, twice 5.

Begin at the bottom righthand corner with a cross, representing one bead. The square next to the cross is left blank. This is repeated four times so that the row is made up of 5 crosses and 5 blanks. In the second row, the first square is left blank and the second marked with a cross and this too is repeated 4 times, so that each blank is above a cross and each cross above a blank. Continue for about 3/4", with each x representing a bead in the basic colour of the band. After that, begin to introduce a different colour, or colours, to make up a pattern. Two designs are shown here.

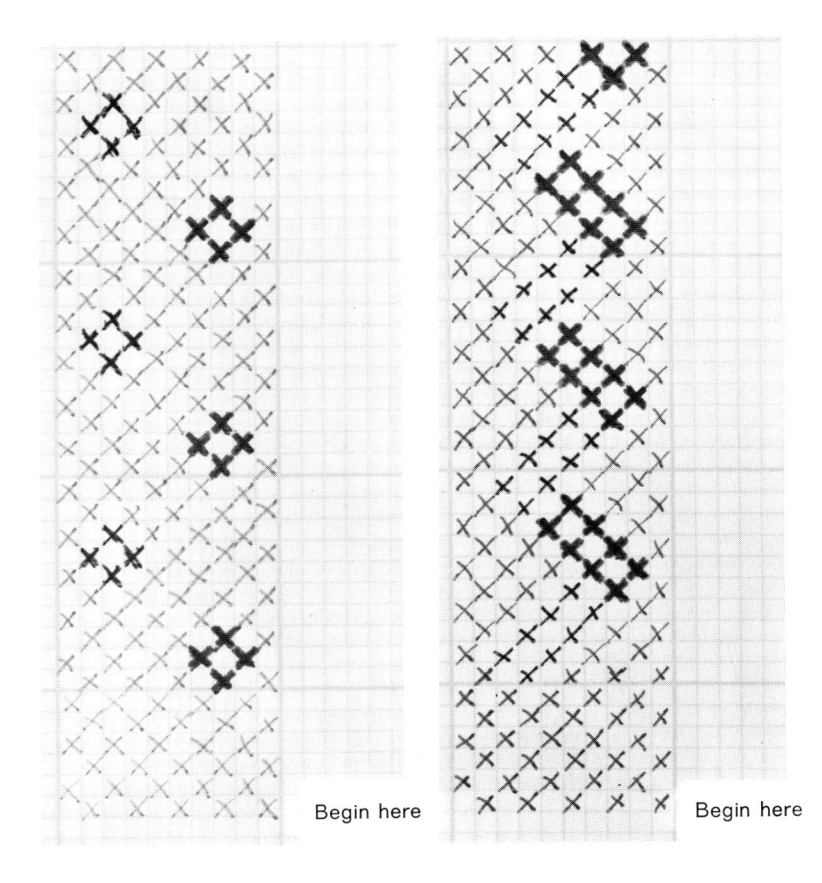

Begin here   Begin here

In addition, it is often helpful to make a note in the margin, showing the beads required for each row.

blue = b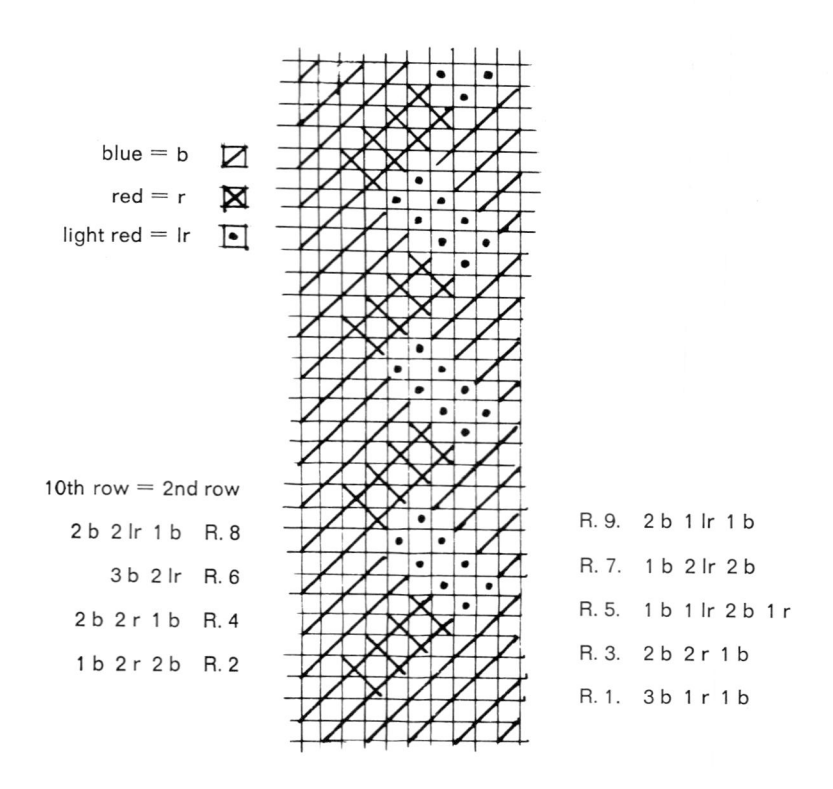

red = r

light red = lr

10th row = 2nd row

2 b 2 lr 1 b   R. 8

3 b 2 lr   R. 6

2 b 2 r 1 b   R. 4

1 b 2 r 2 b   R. 2

R. 9.   2 b 1 lr 1 b

R. 7.   1 b 2 lr 2 b

R. 5.   1 b 1 lr 2 b 1 r

R. 3.   2 b 2 r 1 b

R. 1.   3 b 1 r 1 b

Owing to the alternate spacing of the beads, diagonal designs lend themselves more readily to this work.

At the present time, beadwork is widely used in South America and also the Near East, for souvenirs for the tourist trade. The handsome serpent on the back cover of this book comes from Greece.

Summer handbags made with
wooden beads

40

The making of beadwork mats in a simple pattern has often been one of the handicrafts taught in primary schools. This type of beadwork has now been adapted for modern summer handbags. Here again, complete kits are obtainable, containing the beads as well as ready-sewn lining and frame.

The bag illustrated below has a brown teak frame with green wooden beads. The thread is taken double and the beads are sewn so that each four form a square (diagram overleaf).

Handbag with teak frame

1st row: Join the ends of the thread in a stout knot and string 4 beads. Form them into a square by re-threading the needle through the first and second beads. Then, for extra strength, take the thread through the whole square again before going on to the next square. Work 11 squares in all. At the end of the row, the thread should be between the second and third bead of the last square.

In the following row, each two beads forming a V, or a half-square, are joined with two new beads to make up a complete square. The principle is as follows: —

Thread the needle through bead 4 of the last square and through bead 3 of the next square. Take up 2 new beads and complete the square by drawing the needle once more through the two first beads threaded.

2nd row: Draw thread through bead 3 of the last square of row 1 and complete row as described.

3rd row: Turn work. Re-thread bead 3 of the last square worked. Take up 3 new beads, join into a square with the last bead re-threaded. Then continue as before.

4th row: Turn work. Re-thread bead 4 from the last square of row 2, thread 3 new beads and close square by once more re-threading bead 4 of the last row. Then re-thread beads 2 and 3 of the new square and continue to the end of the row.

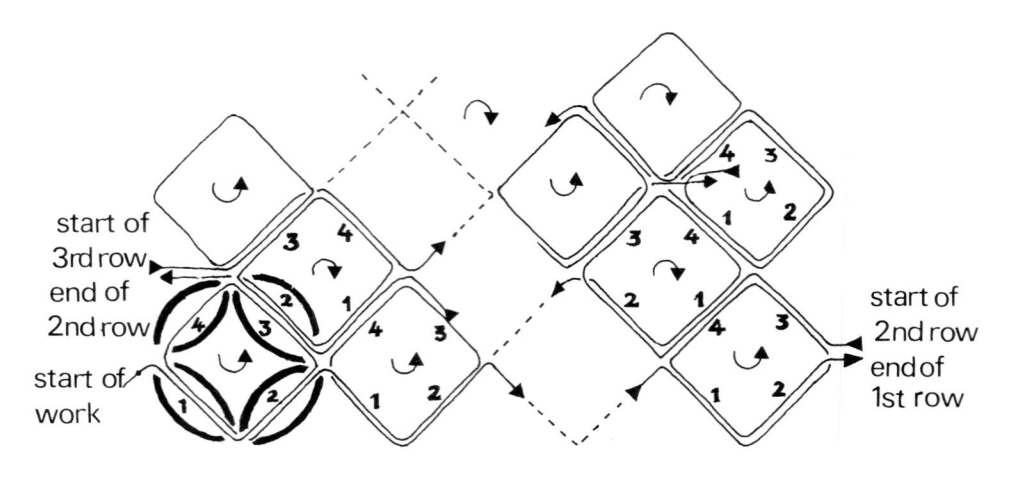

Work a total of 43 rows. Rows 3 and 4 are constantly repeating themselves. The work will accordingly be 22 squares long which, folded in half, gives a finished bag 11 by 11 squares. When the thread runs out, join it to a new one with a weaver's knot. The joint should be sufficiently close to a bead to allow knot and ends to be concealed inside the bead.

Making up: Fold in half and join to a depth of 7 squares. Again, each two half-squares are made into a complete one, as described. The edges left open are reinforced by re-threading. The ready-to-use lining is fitted into the bag so that half a square extends beyond the top. The wooden handle is stitched to the lining.

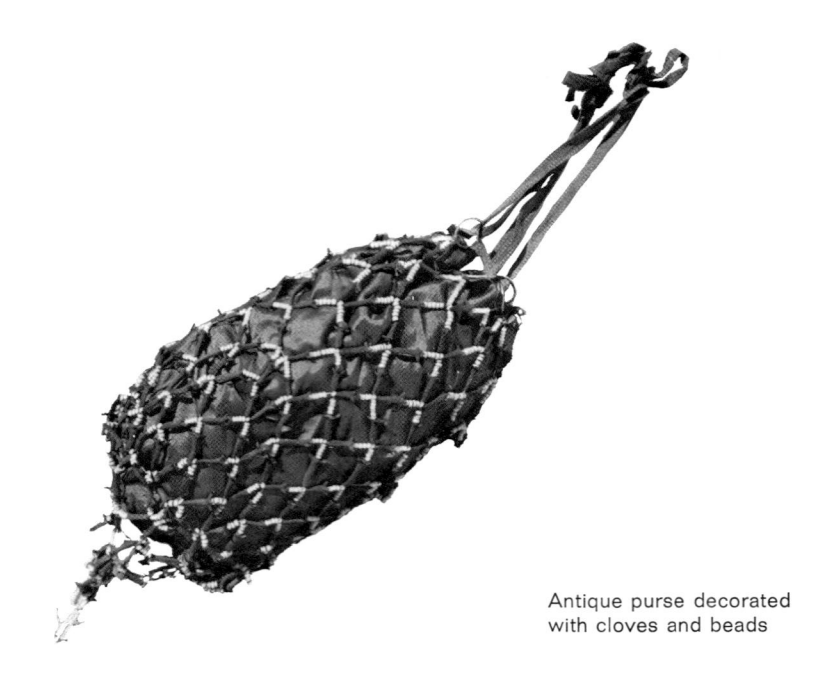

Antique purse decorated
with cloves and beads

Similar beadwork was done 100 years ago. The picture shows a 100-year old purse on which an inventive needlewoman has embroidered perforated cloves between the beads. The use of fragrant whole spices was one of the crazes of that time. The ladies even embroidered small pictures with garlands of spices arranged on white silk.

This chapter would not be complete without a reference to the simple necklace, and the stringing of beads. Perhaps, though, simple is not quite the word — the craft represents a challenge not only to the amateur but also to many professionals whose work is concerned with beads or pearls. Here again, the only tools required are strong thread and a thin needle. Only one example of this work is shown — a necklace of black and white glass beads with matching ear-rings. The necklace consists of 15 thin strings of beads in irregular colour sequence. The ends are joined to a clasp. The ear-rings are worked in a similar way.

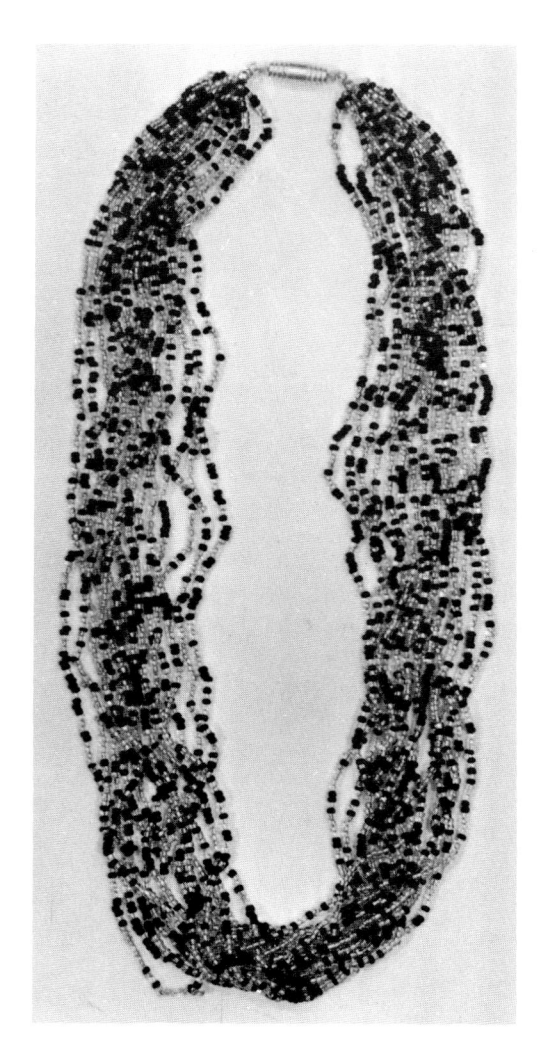

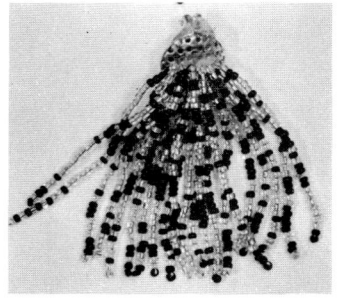

EMBROIDERY WITH CRYSTALS

Embroidery with shimmering crystals is quite a new form of handicraft and one that is fascinating and attractive. Until recently, this form of embroidery was associated only with the grand evening dresses of the Haute Couture, but the fashion has now spread to the home dressmaker. Glitter is no longer confined to evening or cocktail dresses. Crystals are found on accessories, scarves, stoles, gloves, collars and cuffs and, of course, handbags, even on shoes. Dedicated knitters, who have never yet been daunted by any fashion, are using crystals to decorate evening tops or cardigans, and so make their own contribution to fashion.

Crystals are available in a variety of colours and shapes, and some have charming names. Depending on their shape, they are known as

Rosettes	Discs
Marguerites	Drops
Rondels	Set roses
Tubes	

They are available in the following colours: —

clear glass	red
iridescent crystal	green
black	golden yellow
blue	

Some specialist shops supply handy packets, containing a given number of these crystals in the colour required, together with the corresponding number of small white glass beads (Rocaille beads) used to keep the crystals in place.

Rosettes, marguerites and discs have a hole in the centre. To fasten them to the fabric, insert the needle from wrong side at the point selected, thread first the crystal, then the rocaille bead, and pull (a). Return needle through the hole in the crystal, this time from the right side (b). Pull thread, so that the bead is at the top and keeps the crystal in place (c). In the paillette embroidery of earlier days, it used to be necessary to return the thread across one side of the disk. The visible thread had then to be covered by the next paillette. In modern crystal embroidery, the tiny bead obviates the need to take the thread across the crystal.

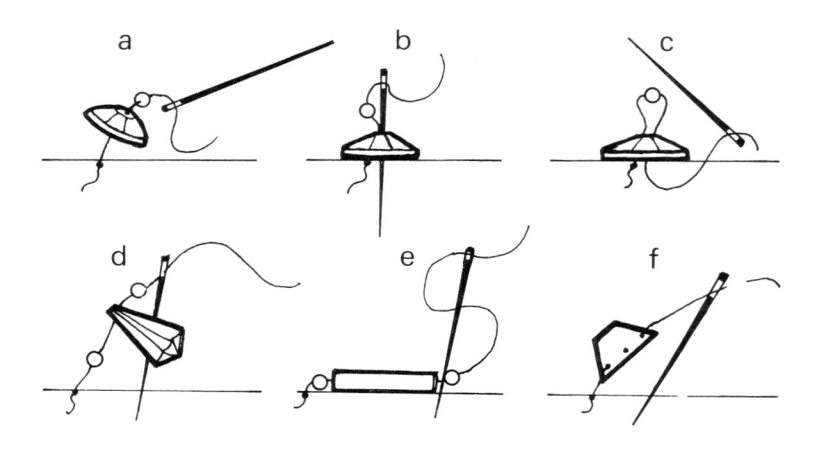

The pretty drops (pendants) are affixed with two rocaille beads. Insert the needle from the wrong side of the fabric, thread through one bead, then through the hole in the drop, then through the second bead, and finally back through the fabric (d). The two beads further prevent chafing of the thread by the relatively heavy crystal. The same technique is used for the tubes but they can be affixed without beads.
Crystals in a metal setting, which has two openings, and round crystal beads, are applied without the use of rocaille beads (f).

Crystal embroidery is governed by much the same principles as bead embroidery. The tools are a fine needle, a threader and a thimble. The thread should be very strong and lasting. Synthetics or pure silk are recommended. The durability of the thread is of even greater importance than for beadwork, as the crystals are slightly heavier. The final effect depends on precise placing. For the same reason, a firm base is required. Thin, slippery material should be taken double or backed with Vilene or a similar fabric. As in bead embroidery, the stitches connecting crystals on the wrong side should not be too long. Here again, the completed work should be lightly lined on the wrong side, both to neaten it and to protect the threads.

The ground fabric may be plain or patterned. A pattern means that much of the design work has been done. All that is required to enrich the fabric is to place some crystals of a suitable colour at some appropriate points of the pattern. This form of embroidery makes a higher demand on imagination and colour sense than on drawing ability.

A plain fabric calls for a proper design. It is a good idea to experiment by arranging crystals on a scrap of fabric, before committing the design to paper, actual size. The design is then transferred to the fabric by pouncing or tracing. With dark or very smooth fabrics, such as satin, or with velvet, this is not possible. In such a case, the drawing should be transferred to tissue paper, which is then tacked to the fabric. The crystals are sewn on through the tissue paper, which is carefully pulled off when the work id completed.

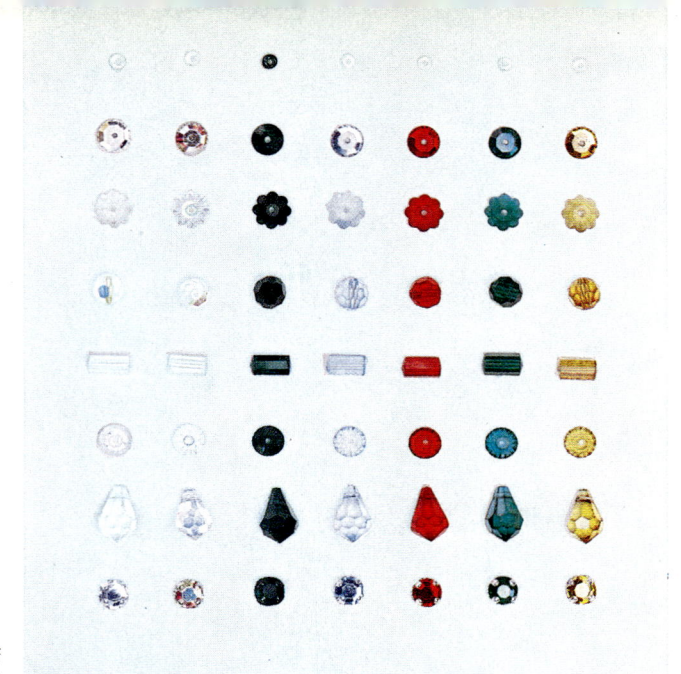

An assortment of
crystals — shapes and
colours to choose from

Evening handbag with knitted-in gold-coloured glass beads

A first attempt at crystal embroidery should not be too ambitious —
perhaps some accessory.
Simple motifs arranged in horizontal or vertical lines provide a
delicate yet effective decoration. A few examples shown below may
help with design work.

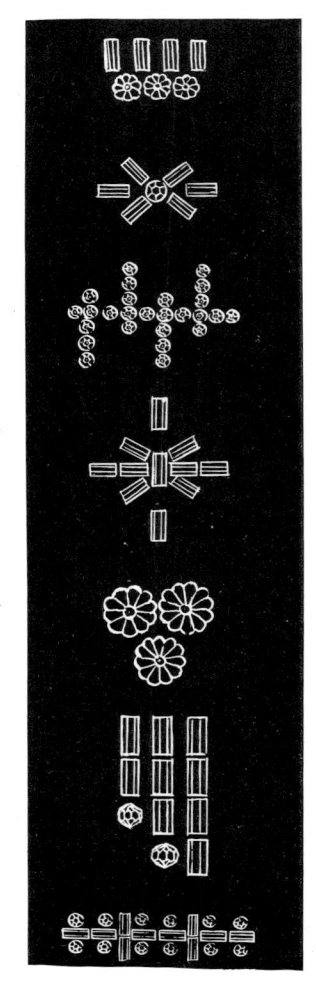

3 marguerites fastened with rocaille
beads. Interspaced above are, 4 tubes.

6 tube-shaped beads radiating from a
round bead. Particularly attractive in a
single colour and in iridescent stones.

Rosettes only. Careful drawing is essential for maximum effect.

Tubes only. Even sewing is seential for
this design. When tightening the thread,
the tube must be eased into just the
right position.

3 slightly larger marguerites (6 mm or
1/4"). Easier to work.

The same applies to this rather severe
motif consisting of 9 tube-shaped beads
and 2 round beads.

Tubes and rondels combined to form a
delicate, multi-purpose border.

Handbags to match the evening dress.
You can embroider them with crystals and fit
them yourself with lining and frame.

A geometrical design of rosettes only. A rather more striking border, suitable for the hem of a dress.

In this design, most of the tubes are horizontal. Here again, the work must be very even. If used on a belt, for example, the motifs should be embroidered pointing alternately up and down.

The two adjacent designs can be used to cover an area, such as the top of an evening dress. Tubes and rosettes, or rosettes and drops, may be used. Rocaille beads scattered or in small groups enhance the effect.

A similar effect is produced by these designs of rosettes and droplets, suitable for striking embroidery on rich materials, such as velvet.

These two designs can be worked in rosettes, rondels or marguerites. They have attractive, clean lines but demand great skill.

The question of where to use crystal embroidery is essentially a matter of personal preference. Here are a few suggestions. These belts are made up of the same material as the dress, and the designs are embroidered close together. Belts should have a firm backing as well as a lining. Crystal embroidery belts are a fashionable decoration for evening dresses of simple design. An embroidered belt can revitalise a dress that has remained in the wardrobe for rather a long time.

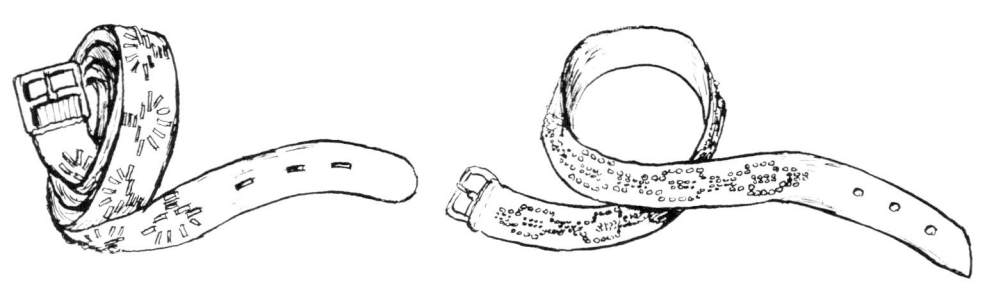

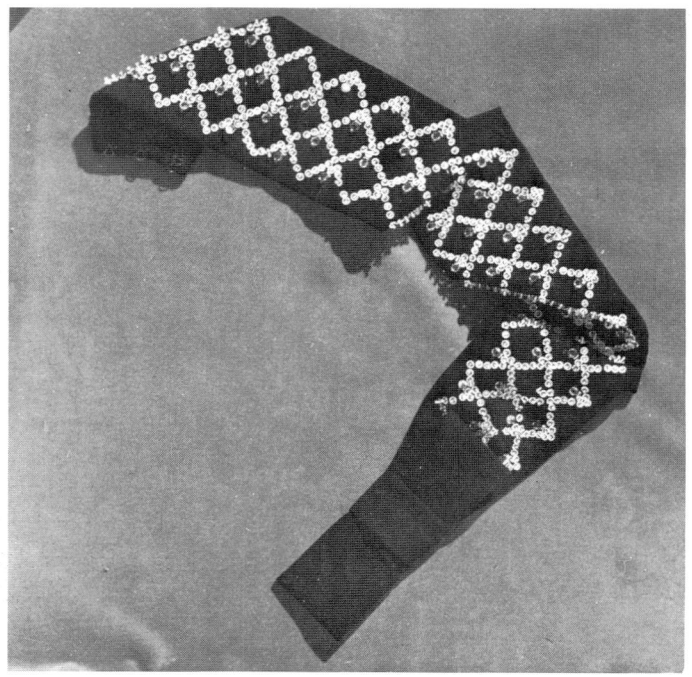

The designs suggested here can be used for a wide border on a scarf, or a more delicate one for evening gloves. They can also be adapted for collars and cuffs.

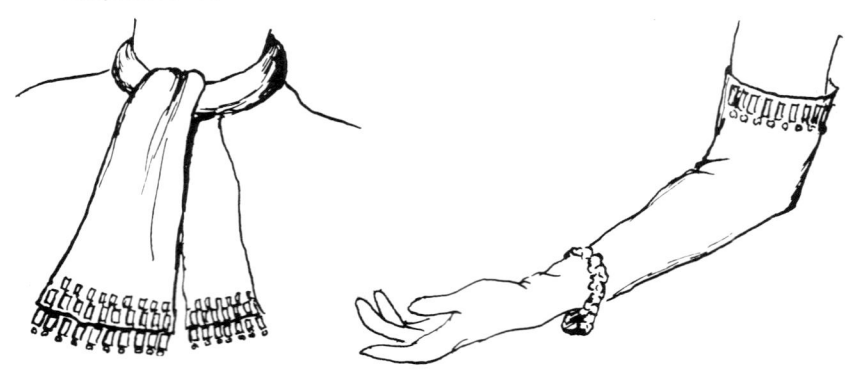

Beginners get special pleasure from embroidering an evening bag, which can be bought complete in an attractive kit. The kit consists of fabric, frame, ready-sewn lining, the right number of crystals and rocaille beads and, most important of all, the complete design on tissue paper. The paper is tacked to the fabric. The beads are sewn on through the paper which is later pulled off.

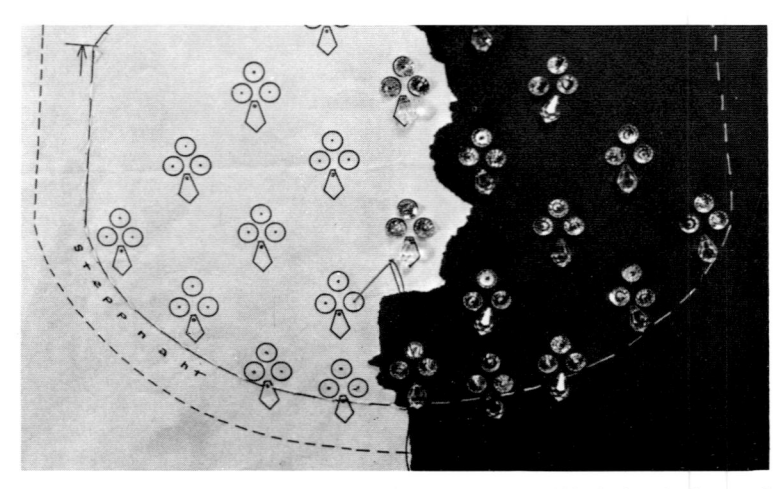

Work detail of crystal
embroidery through paper

The two illustrations below show completed simple designs consisting of tubes and rosettes. The next four designs are a little more difficult as tubes predominate. Tubes must be carefully placed and secured, and a suitable backing is essential. The practical uses of crystal embroidery are demonstrated with a belt for a full-length evening dress (p. 54). The belt is embroidered on heavy wool georgette reinforced with Vilene. After completion of the embroidery, the belt was lined with the same georgette. The large number of closely placed rosettes makes the belt somewhat heavy but the effect is striking.

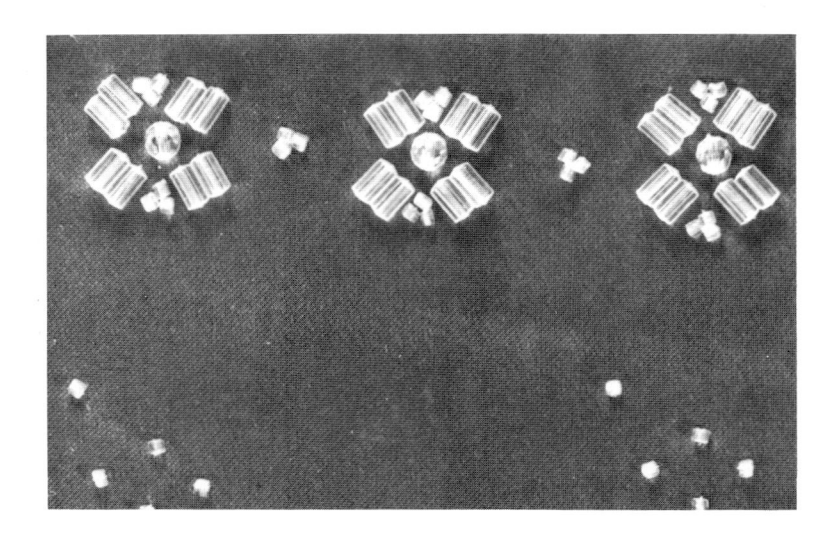

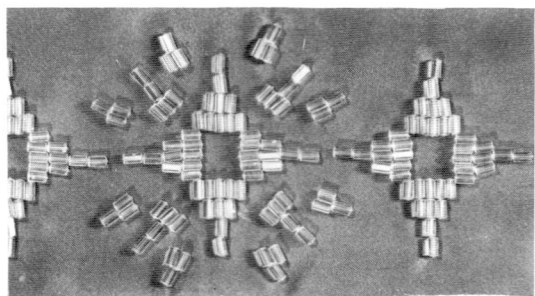

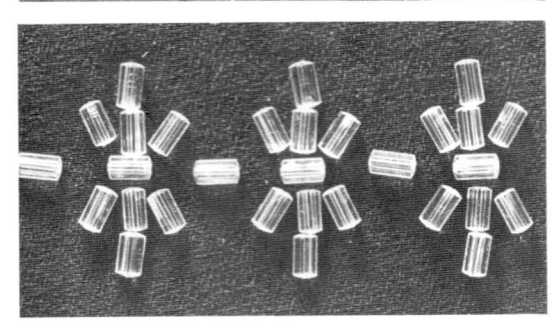

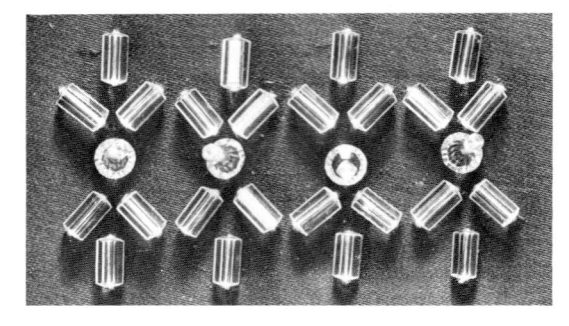

Full-length black evening
gown with crystal embroidery belt

Meander pattern. This border, which calls for practice and skill, was drawn in full on tissue paper which was then tacked to an evening dress of violet coloured velvet. It covers the front seams and mandarin collar.

Design of border in crystal embroidery

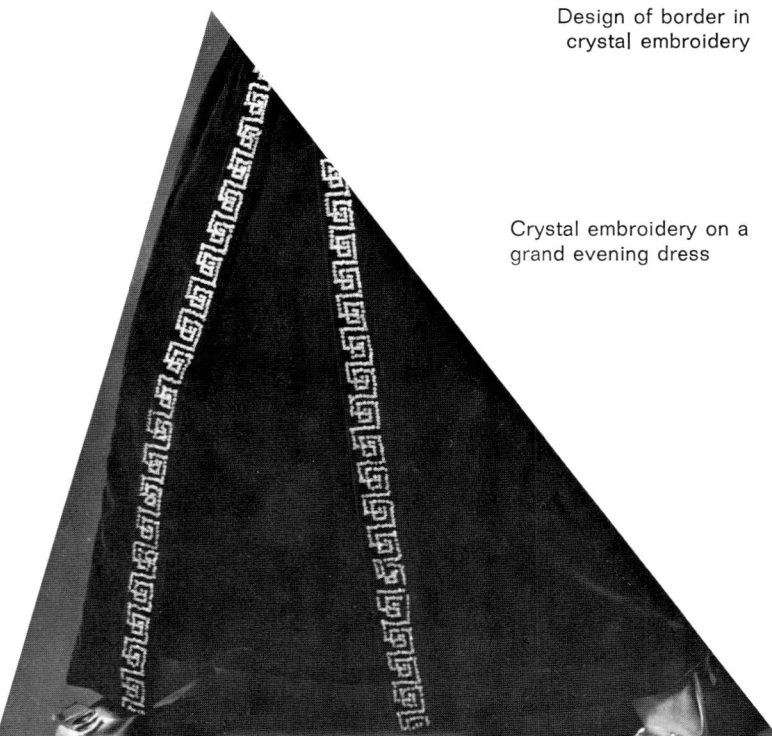

Crystal embroidery on a grand evening dress

Quite a new use for crystal embroidery is in the decoration of knitted rather than woven fabric. Where possible, the knitting pattern should be chosen with embroidery in mind. Suitable patterns are those with a repetitive design but not too chunky (no cable stitch etc.). All that is then left to decide is which parts of an evening top or cardigan are to be embroidered with crystals. If liked, the entire area of an evening top may be covered. It is obviously important to choose crystals that blend well with the colour of the working thread. This, in turn, should be of the right texture. Double-knit wools are obviously unsuitable. Delicate crochet yarns in pastel shades, pure wool or synthetic fibres go well with iridescent stones or beads, or with clear crystals. Yarns with Lurex enhance the final effect.

The following knitting patterns may be found useful as a basis for crystal embroidery.

The first pattern is knitted in light green wool. The crystal beads are embroidered on little nests of purled stitches.

The number of stitches cast on must be divisible by three (plus 2 end stitches).

1st row: Knit, plain.

2nd row: Purl.

3rd row: Knit, plain.

4th row: Purl 3. For each of the next 3, pierce the stitch immediately below, leave on needle and purl together with normal stitch. Purl 3 and so on.

5th row: Knit plain.

6th row: Purl.

7th row: Knit plain.

8th row: as 4th row, but move nest on three stitches.

Another evening cardigan, of bright yellow man-made fibre with a striped pattern, is subsequently embroidered on the fronts with iridescent rosettes.

Work some rows in stocking stitch in the required width. Then:

1st row: Purl 2, lift off 1, draw wool across needle, purl 2 and continue to the end of the row.

2nd row: Purl 2, lift off the same stitch lifted off in the last row, draw wool across so that there now are 1 stitch and 2 lifted-off threads on the needle, purl 2. Repeat to the end of the row.

3rd row: purl only, including the lifted-off stitches together with the threads.

To frame the stripes, work some rows in stocking stitch.

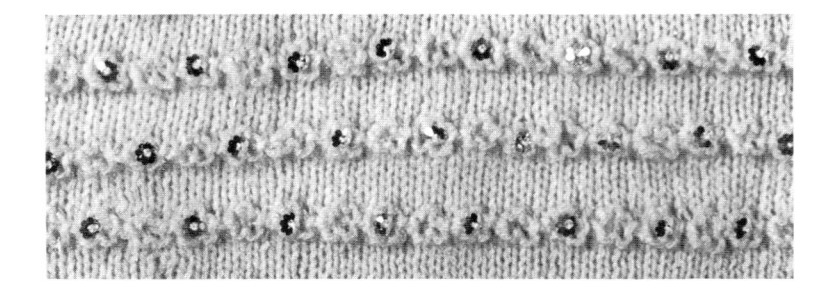

The cast-on stitches do in fact form the side seams, so that the stripes are vertical. Subsequently an iridescent rosette is embroidered into every other rosette formed by the knitting pattern.

The bow pattern is also well suited to crystal embroidery. The suggested colour scheme for an evening cardigan is fine silver-grey wool with Lurex thread, and rosettes and drops in clear crystal.

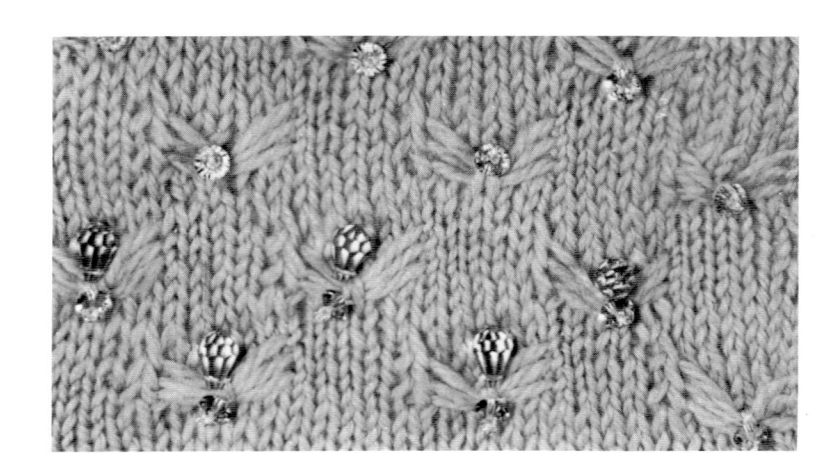

The number of stitches cast on must be divisible by 5 (+2 end stitches).

1st row: Knit 5, lift off 5, pull thread in front of needle, knit 5, repeat to end of row.

(NB. The instructions are again based on the Continental style of knitting.)

2nd row: (wrong side) purl only.

3rd row: as 1st row.

4th row: as 2nd row.

5th row: as 1st row.

6th row: as 2nd row.

7th row: knit 5, then knit 2, lift the 3rd stitch from the left to the right needle, pick up the 3 cross threads from the row below and knit together with stitch. Knit 9, then repeat, picking up in the centre of the next group of threads.

8th row: purl only.

9th row: as 1st row, but move on pattern by 5 stitches. In other words, begin by lifting off 5.

A fancy waistcoat is knitted in stocking stitch in dark green wool and embroidered with red crystal rosettes grouped to form larger rosettes. Rosettes set in metal may also be used.

Fancy waistcoat with
crystal embroidery   59

Crochet patterns too can be designed as a base for embroidery. A turquoise evening top may be embroidered with round crystal beads. Each bead forms the centre of a crocheted flower.

Begin with a length of chain stitch. For the pattern, work as follows: —

1st row: 3 chains for turning, 1 Tr into the 4th ch, 2 ch, miss 2 ch, 1 DC into the next chain, 2 ch, miss 2 ch, (+) 1 Tr into the next ch, pull up loop about 1 cm (½") loop round, twist round the last Tr crocheted from front to back. Draw up working loop, loop round, twist again, draw up working loop, loop round, miss 2 ch, insert hook into next ch, pull up loop ½", loop round, insert hook, pull up, loop round, insert hook, pull up, miss 2 ch, loop around, insert hook, pull up, loop round, insert hook into same spot, pull up, loop round, insert hook into same spot, pull through all the loops on the crochet hook and finish with 1 ch. Pull up working thread ½", loop round, insert hook, pull up, loop round, insert hook, pull up, loop round, insert hook, pull up, draw working thread through all the loops, and join them with 1 chain, 2 ch, miss 2 ch, 1 Tr, 2 ch, miss 2 ch, 1 DC, 2 ch, miss 2 ch, 1 Tr. Repeat from (+).

2nd row: 3 ch for turning, 1 Tr into the Tr below, 2 ch, 1 DC into the DC below, 2 ch, 1 Tr into Tr below, (+) 2 ch, loop round, insert hook into centre of flower below, pull up working loop ½", loop round, insert hook, pull up, loop round, insert hook, pull up, draw working thread through all the loops, join in 1 ch, loop round, insert hook, pull up, loop round, insert hook, pull up, loop round, insert hook, pull up, draw working thread through all loops, join in 1 ch, 2 ch, 1 Tr attached by going round the Tr of previous row, 2 ch, 1 DC, 2 ch, 1 Tr. Repeat from (+).

3rd row: 3 ch to turn. 1 Tr into the Tr below, then work as 1st row from (+) except that the Tr is inserted into the Tr below and the second and third flowers are now inserted to the right and left of the double crochet below.

4th row: As 2nd row.

This somewhat complicated pattern is an example of many flower and leaf designs that lend themselves particularly well to embroidery.

For the more experienced needlewoman, there are exciting designs combining crystal decoration with other forms of embroidery. The illustration below shows one such combination. An arrangement of rosettes and beads on green wool georgette is combined with lea-

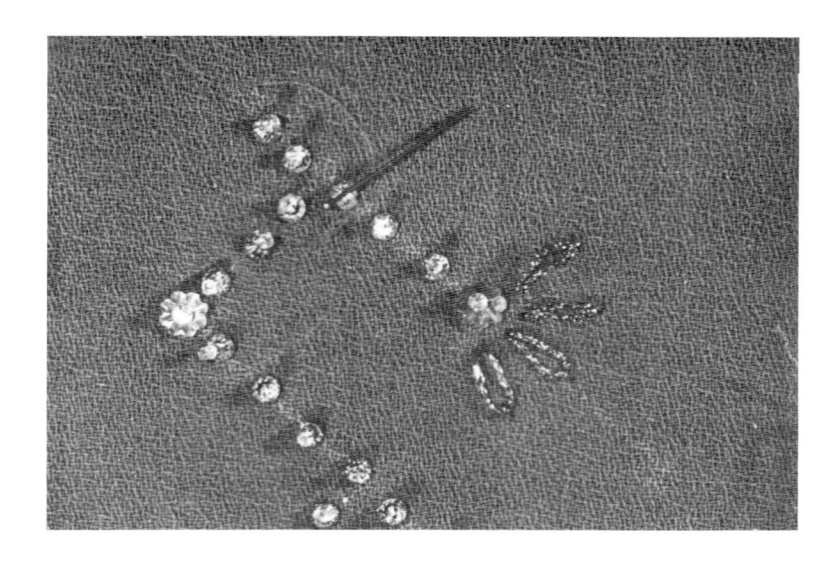

ves, embroidered in detached chain-stitch with gold thread. — Below, light brown and dark brown motifs are embroidered in satin stitch on gold-coloured silk. The effect is enhanced by the addition of small dark brown beads and golden-yellow crystals.

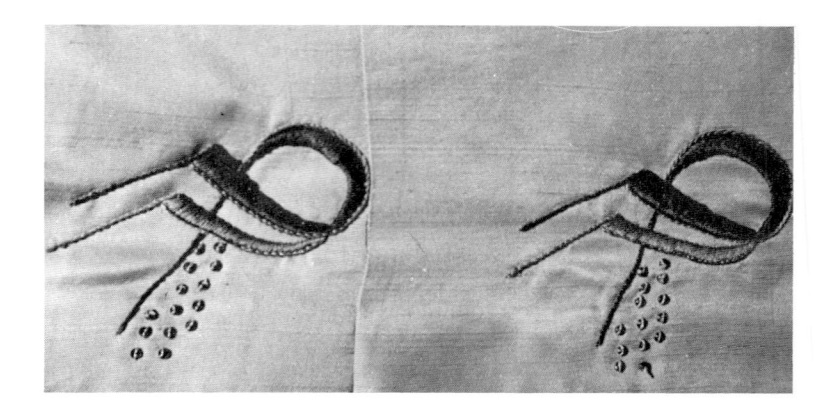

The next design combines imagination and draughtsmanship, in that the fabric is first painted with special colours and then embroidered with crystals. A stylised garland of green leaves is painted on beige wool georgette. The colours are fixed by ironing on the wrong side, after which small, round white beads and yellow and red crystals are added.

Green leaves painted in fabric

colours Crystals:

- mother-of-pearl
- ruby
- yellow
  milk glass

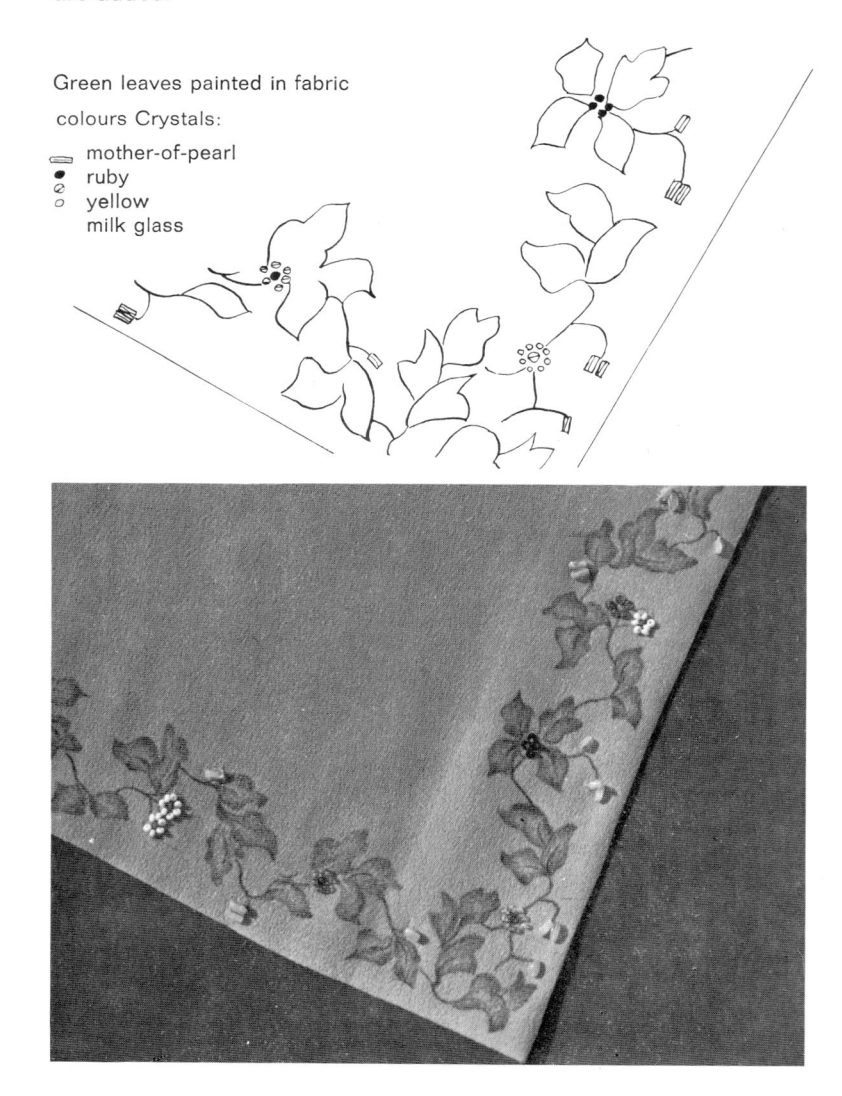

The examples, together with the knitting and crochet patterns contained in this book, are intended to do no more than introduce the
various forms and techniques of bead and crystal embroidery.
It is left to the initiative and creative ability of each needlewoman to
find new and still more attractive uses for this charming and delicate
craft.

Acknowledgments:
The author and publishers wish to thank
D. Swarovski & Co., Wattens, Tyrol
VARIATA, (D. Lang) Mühlacker
Geyer & Co., Leibener Wollgarnspinnerei, Leiben, N. Austria
for the illustrations made available.

The author also thanks Fr. Leni Wolter, Hanau, for special advice
on needle weaving with beads.